In loving memory of my father, Mr Malik Abdul Razzak
and for my mother Mrs Zaiba Razzak – S.R.

Huge thanks to Imran Khan; Tanweer, Kaikishan and their families
and friends in Karachi; Mr Suhail and friends in Lahore; Aazam,
Abdul Aziz, Islam Khan and Younus Khan in Peshawar, and
the many children in Pakistan who were a joy to work with – P.D.

P is for Pakistan copyright © Frances Lincoln Limited 2007
Text copyright © Shazia Razzak 2007
Photographs copyright © Prodeepta Das 2007
The Publishers would like to acknowledge Ifeoma Onyefulu as the originator
of the series of which this book forms a part. Ifeoma Onyefulu is the author
and photographer of *A is for Africa*.

First published in Great Britain and the USA in 2007
by Frances Lincoln Children's Books, 4 Torriano Mews,
Torriano Avenue, London NW5 2RZ
www.franceslincoln.com

Distributed in the USA by Publishers Group West

British Library Cataloguing in Publication Data available on request

ISBN: 978-184507-483-8

Printed in Singapore

1 3 5 7 9 8 6 4 2

P is for Pakistan

Shazia Razzak ❖ Prodeepta Das

F

FRANCES LINCOLN
CHILDREN'S BOOKS

AUTHOR'S NOTE

I was born in Rawalpindi, near Islamabad, in the Punjab province of Pakistan. Every time I revisit the country, I am touched by people's friendliness, warmth and willingness to help.

Pakistan is a developing country with a lot to offer, from bright, colourful, noisy cities to quiet, custom-bound villages. The main religion practised is Islam, but some people follow Christianity, Hinduism and Sikhism. Pakistan's provinces include the Punjab, Sindh, Balochistan and the North West Frontier Province. In each province you will find differences in the way people live and the language they speak, as well as the style of clothes they wear. It is these differences that give Pakistan its colourful personality.

This book sets out to give a true flavour of the people and how they live. I hope it will encourage young people to discover more about Pakistan and perhaps one day to visit this fascinating country.

Shazia Razzak

Aa

is for Asslam-U-Alaikum.

This is how people in Pakistan say hello!

Bb

is for Badshahi Mosque, in the city of Lahore. Many people come here to pray, and to admire its beauty. At night it is lit up, giving it an amazing and enchanting glow.

Cc

is for Charpaye, a traditional village bed with a wooden or metal frame. It is woven with colourful yarns in many different patterns. By day it is a place to sit and talk, and at night it becomes a bed to sleep on and dream.

Dd

is for Dhobi ghat, an open-air laundry near the river bank, where dhobis – washermen and women – bring all the town's dirty clothes to wash and spread out to dry.

Ee

is for Eid, two of the year's most important Islamic celebrations.
Eid-Ul-Fitre marks the end of Ramadan, the month of fasting,
and Eid-Ul-Addha is celebrated after Hajj, the pilgrimage to Mecca.
Girls give each other bangles and decorate their hands with henna.
Families feast together, give presents, and say special prayers at
the mosque to celebrate.

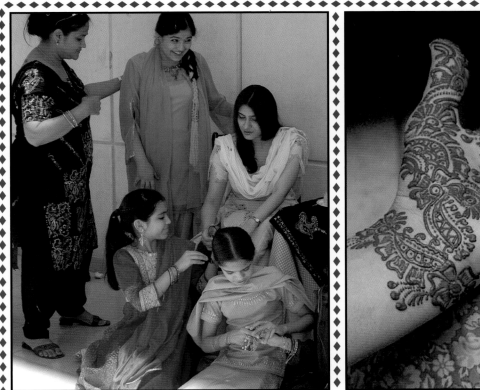

 is for the wonderful Fruits grown all over Pakistan. In spring and after summer mangoes, bananas and watermelons come into season, while in autumn and after the winter oranges, dates and guava can be found everywhere. Bhere, the fruit being bought here, is used to make sauces.

Gg

is for Ghar, our home. A family home can be a big mansion in the city, a small house on the plain or a simple village hut in the mountains. Pakistani people live together in extended families made up of children, parents, grandparents and sometimes aunts and uncles too!

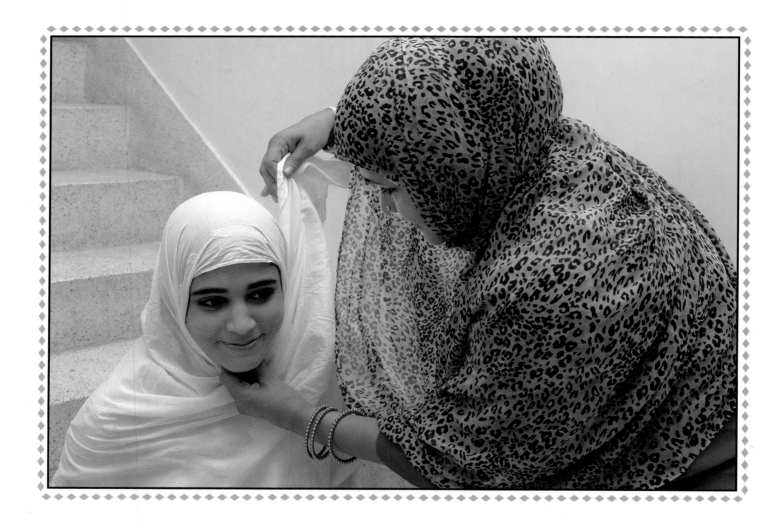

Hh

is for Hijaab, which means dressing modestly. Most Muslim women wear a headscarf to cover their hair, ears and throat. Others cover their whole body except for the eyes.

 is for Indus, the big, big river flowing all the way from the north to the south of Pakistan. Some of the earliest cities grew up along its banks four thousand years ago. Now that dams have been built upstream to give electricity, the mighty river has become very dry.

Jj

is for Jasmine, the national flower of Pakistan. We have used it to make perfume for hundreds of years. Its fragrance is strongest in the evening. Street sellers in the cities carry jasmine bangles on sticks.

Kk

is for Kulfi – a special ice-cream much creamier than ordinary ice-cream, which we buy from kulfi stands and kulfi parlours. Our favourite flavours are strawberry, banana, pistachio and mango.

is for Laddu – sweet balls made from chickpea flour and sugar. Some laddus are made from coconut with almonds and other nuts. We often give them as presents on happy occasions such as birthdays and Eid.

Mm

is for Mothi – sequins and beads used to embroider scarves, shirts and dresses. Mothis come in many beautiful colours, shapes and sizes and we also use them to make jewellery.

Nn

is for Nihari, a spicy meat curry we eat with Naan, a soft round bread. It is a great favourite in Karachi and Lahore restaurants.

Oo

is for Ointment, which we buy from the herbalist. In many parts of Pakistan, herbalists are more popular than doctors and are often much cheaper. People sometimes travel great distances to consult a good herbalist.

Pp is for Pakistan, a country born in 1947. Its people speak many languages including English, Punjabi, Pushto and Sindhi, but Urdu is the official language. Islamabad is the capital city, and there are many bustling towns and quiet villages as well as beautiful mountains, lakes, rivers and deserts.

Qq

is for Qawali, songs of Islam. Qawali singers are usually accompanied by a tambourine, a harmonium and a tabla (a small drum). They sing for hours, starting late at night and going on into the early morning.

Rr

is for Rickshaw, a kind of taxi which has been converted from a three-wheeled motorbike to carry passengers.

Ss

is for Shalwar-Kameez, a three-piece suit made up of a long blouse, trousers and a scarf or shawl. Each region has its own style of outfit. Women and girls wear them every day, and like to dress up in their most glamorous shalwar-kameez with matching handbags and shoes for weddings and special occasions.

Tt

is for Truck, covered with lively poems and decorated all over with bright, colourful paintings. They are one of the most exciting forms of folk art in Pakistan.

Uu

is for Urdu, our national language.
It is full of charm and elegance.
We write it from right to left.

Vv

is for Volleyball, a game played by two
teams of six who volley the ball back
and forth over a net with their hands.
Like cricket, it is very popular and
tournaments are played all over
the country.

Ww

is for Water buffaloes, who look more terrifying than they really are. They like to laze in water all day long.

 **Xx** is for the eXciting kite festival of Basant which marks the coming of spring. On rooftops and on the beach, people of all ages gather to fly kites of every size and colour.

Yy

is for Yaar, the Urdu word for friends, who greet each other with hugs and handshakes.

Zz

is for Zeewar, or jewellery.
People like to show off their gold
at weddings and parties. Nowadays
we often wear modern costume
jewellery, which looks just as
attractive as traditional jewellery.